Designing Your
WOMEN'S
MINISTRY

A Step-By-Step
Planning Guide

Loveland, Colorado

Group resources really work!

This Group resource incorporates our R.E.A.L. approach to ministry. It reinforces a growing friendship with Jesus, encourages long-term learning, and results in life transformation, because it's:

Relational—Learner-to-learner interaction enhances learning and builds Christian friendships.

Experiential—What learners experience through discussion and action sticks with them up to 9 times longer than what they simply hear or read.

Applicable—The aim of Christian education is to equip learners to be both hearers and doers of God's Word.

Learner-based—Learners understand and retain more when the learning process takes into consideration how they learn best.

DESIGNING YOUR Women's Ministry
A Step-by-Step Planning Guide

Visit our website: **group.com/women**

Unless otherwise indicated, all Scripture quotations are taken from the *Holy Bible*, New Living Translation, copyright © 1996, 2004, 2007, 2013 by Tyndale House Foundation. Used by permission of Tyndale House Publishers, Inc., Carol Stream, Illinois 60188. All rights reserved.

ISBN 978-1-4707-2306-4
Printed in the United States of America

10 9 8 7 6 5 4 3 2 1   24 23 22 21 20 19 18 17 16 15

Contents

It's Time to Design! 4

A Firm Foundation 7

Building a Team 17

Making a Design Plan 23

Designed to Work as a Team 37

An Energy-Efficient Design 53

Open House! 61

Spread the Word! 67

Designed for Relationship With God 75

Designed for Relationships With Others 85

Designed for All Ages 93

Celebrating Success! 107

IT'S TIME TO Design!

When was the last time you did a bit of redesign in your home? Perhaps you got new cushions for your couch. Repainted a few walls. Installed a different color of carpet. Or maybe you started over and knocked out walls, rebuilt new ones, and changed the layout entirely. Or you might have decided the old house wasn't worth fixing and decided to start completely from the ground up, hiring an architect to create new plans for an entirely new home.

It can be a lot of fun to change things up and refresh our living spaces. But what about your ministry? When was the last time you did a bit of redesign? Have you successfully made changes within the last year? Or have you been doing the exact same women's ministry program for 5, 10, or even 50 years? It's time to refresh and design a women's ministry that meets the needs of today's women!

We're here to help! Through this easy-to-use resource, we'll walk you through the steps to either start an incredible women's ministry in your church or make your current women's ministry better than ever.

We've walked alongside thousands of women's ministry leaders just like you and have learned a lot in the process. We've put that knowledge to work for you here, so there's no guesswork involved. Within these pages you'll find just what you need to set a firm foundation, raise sturdy structures, and design a ministry that's relevant for women—all while drawing them closer to God.

How to Use This Book

This book is created to be used as a workbook. You'll write in the pages, adding your own thoughts, ideas, and plans. We highly recommend you work through this with a team—but if you're alone in ministry at this point, don't let that stop you. As you work through the pages, you'll find help on how to invite others into your ministry leadership team. So if you have a team, **make sure everyone has her own copy of this book** and set aside time on a weekly or monthly basis to work through this step by step. If it's just you, start at the beginning and know you'll be finding help soon!

The book is roughly divided into two sections. The first part of the book focuses on the foundations of your ministry, including mission and leadership. The second part of the book focuses on the implementation of programs and the actual day-to-day with the women in your church and community. You'll start with the foundation—and then move into application of this in your ministry.

Let's get started!

A FIRM Foundation

Any builder will tell you that the key to a strong and long-standing structure is a firm foundation. The Bible repeats this as well, letting us know that a firm, foundational relationship with Jesus is what will keep us strong in the storms of life. It's the same with your ministry. You need a firm foundation. No matter what your ministry looks like in the end, you want to start with a strong foundation. What does that look like? There are several components we'll look at here to give you guidance on how to work through this foundation process.

Prayer

It sounds so basic, but prayer is essential. And invite others to pray with you. Partner with a group of women who already meet regularly for prayer or invite several women to pray regularly—alone or together—during a designated day and time. Invite women who are passionate about connecting with God through prayer to walk beside you.

> "They are like a man building a house, who dug down deep and laid the foundation on rock. When a flood came, the torrent struck that house but could not shake it, because it was well built."
>
> —Luke 6:48, NIV

What is my specific prayer for women in our church? our community?

_____

_____

_____

_____

"When I think of all this, I fall to my knees and pray to the Father, the Creator of everything in heaven and on earth. I pray that from his glorious, unlimited resources he will empower you with inner strength through his Spirit. Then Christ will make his home in your hearts as you trust in him. Your roots will grow down into God's love and keep you strong. And may you have the power to understand, as all God's people should, how wide, how long, how high, and how deep his love is. May you experience the love of Christ, though it is too great to understand fully. Then you will be made complete with all the fullness of life and power that comes from God.

"Now all glory to God, who is able, through his mighty power at work within us, to accomplish infinitely more than we might ask or think."

—Ephesians 3:14-20

What is my prayer for women's ministry?

_____

_____

_____

_____

Whom can I invite to pray with me?

_____

_____

_____

_____

After you've invited others to pray with and for you, put a star by those names. And as you see God answering prayers, be sure to return to this page and make notes about those answers and God's direction. You want to be able to celebrate God's hand at work in your ministry!

Support of Leadership

The more your church leaders understand the importance of women's ministry and hear your excitement, the more they'll be willing to support you and your team. To help get you started, consider these leaders as a starting point for sharing your desire to start or redesign your women's ministry:

- Senior pastor
- Any pastor or leader who influences small groups or outreach
- Other pastoral staff
- Administrative assistants
- Wives of any male church leaders
- Elders

Include those whose support is critical for moving forward in your church, but also consider the informal leaders whom others consistently listen to and follow. In some churches you'll need to meet with leaders in a formal way, but in most cases, you can share through casual conversations. Make it a priority to speak with people face to face; your excitement and commitment will show!

Here is a list of people I want to talk to about my passion for women's ministry:

Mission

You also need a foundation in the form of a mission statement. A mission statement articulates what your ministry is about—or what it accomplishes. It's used to help guide decisions about priorities, activities, and responsibilities, and it will help you get others on board with your ministry. If you don't have a mission statement, your women's ministry feels meaningless to others—you can't cast the vision. *You* might get it…but others don't. Having a mission statement will help you as you talk to leaders, it will help you as you move toward recruiting a team, and it will help you decide what to do—and not do—as a ministry.

You can create this statement yourself, but doing it with a few others will likely lead you to the strongest possible mission statement. If you're working through this book solo, you might want to put off creating a mission statement until you've invited one or two others to join you in leading the women's ministry of your church. You can move to the next section of the book, and then come back to the mission as one of the first things you do with those women who are joining you in leadership.

A few things to keep in mind:

 A mission statement needs to be clear to everyone, not just you. If you use lingo or acronyms or Greek words or long words, it will be muddled and hard to explain.

 Keep it short. You want to be able to say it over and over, and you want others to learn it and say it over and over. So make it memorable!

 The Bible can provide good direction! Reflect on the verses we've provided in this section—or others you know—and consider using word or concepts from these.

 Look at the mission statement of your church. You do want to be in alignment with the senior leadership of the church, so see if you can tweak the overarching statement or pull a few key words from it so you're tracking with the rest of the church.

Effective
Mission Statements Are...

- **SIMPLE.** Identify key words important to ministering to your women. Outreach. Care. Growth. Relationships. Community. What are the core values of your church? Prioritize. Can some areas be combined? You can't do it all. Do what you can well.

- **SPECIFIC.** God isn't calling you to the same ministry as the church down the street or on the Internet. Listen to the specific guidance he's giving you. Be obedient and stick to his plan. He knows what he's doing.

- **SHORT.** One phrase or sentence should be sufficient. Women are verbal, and we often want to fit as much as possible. If you feel your mission statement is "stuffed," your ministry to women—and your own schedule—will likely be stuffed. Busy isn't the goal. Effectiveness in ministry is.

"Jesus replied, 'You must love the Lord your God with all your heart, all your soul, and all your mind.' This is the first and greatest commandment. A second is equally important: 'Love your neighbor as yourself.'"

—Matthew 22:37-39

"Therefore, go and make disciples of all the nations, baptizing them in the name of the Father and the Son and the Holy Spirit. Teach these new disciples to obey all the commands I have given you."

—Matthew 28:19-20

"Fix your thoughts on what is true, and honorable, and right, and pure, and lovely, and admirable. Think about things that are excellent and worthy of praise."

—Philippians 4:8

Here are a few mission statements you can consider, along with some comments on what these accomplish. You might want to say "That's it!" and use one of these, or you might want to grapple together with others to determine what's best for your church and ministry. These will at least serve as ideas and a starting point.

We befriend women and give them a place to belong so they'll come to believe in Jesus and become more like him.

👍 This statement speaks toward outreach (befriend), community (belong), faith (believe), and growth (become).

Connecting women to Jesus and one another.

👍 A statement like this puts the focus on Jesus and relationships with other women.

We help women build friendships, encourage women in spiritual growth, and reach out to women in our community with the love of Jesus.

👍 This shows the desire for fellowship, growing relationships with God, and outreach.

To connect women with God, connect women with others, and connect others with God.

👍 Here we see connection as a priority in the areas of faith, fellowship, and in outreach.

To help women experience Christ, grow strong in Christ, and take the Christ-experience to their world.

👍 This statement speaks to a relationship with God—and then taking that to others outside of the church.

🖊 Here are a few words we like and want to keep in mind for our mission:

_____

_____

_____

🖊 Here are Bible verses that have words or ideas we want to incorporate:

_____

_____

_____

🖊 Here are a few possible statements we are thinking about:

_____

_____

_____

This is it! Here is what we have chosen as our mission statement:

We'll be using this statement more in the coming sections, so be sure you write it down. You're going to be using this often!

WHAT SHOULD WE LEAVE OUT?

We've been focusing on what to include in a good foundation...but are there things to leave out? Yes! Leave *competition* and *comparison* behind. Avoid looking at other ministries in your church or other women's ministries at other churches and thinking, "We can be better than them!" Or we might lose hope thinking, "We'll never have as much money (or creativity or staffing or whatever) as they have! We're doomed to fail!"

God wants us to be *for* each other—not *against* each other. We all have the goal of helping women grow closer to God and each other, so let's find ways to partner instead of trying to "one-up" other ministries or give up because we have something different to offer.

DESIGNING YOUR WOMEN'S MINISTRY

Name

We put this last because it's optional. There are a lot of great ministries that just use the name of their church (such as Women's Ministry at First Church or Women of Sunnyside Church or whatever your church's name is). But many women like having a fun name to call their ministry.

Naming is a challenge. Some women like soft and warm names like "Heart to Heart." Others like zippy names like "Sassy Soul Sisters" or "Lemondrop Ladies." Still others like names that reflect Bible or faith interests, such as "Daughters of Destiny" or "Titus 2." So it can be a challenge to come to a consensus.

You do need to capture the character of your ministry—so if you tend toward the soft and warm, it's okay to use a name that reflects that, while if you're an energetic and invigorating group, you'd want to capture that energy instead.

What we advise *against* is choosing a name that alienates women because it's difficult to pronounce (such as a Greek word), or needs an explanation, or requires you're already a Christian to understand it. For example, we wouldn't recommend a name like WIFE (Women In Fellowship and Evangelism) because it implies it's only for married women—thus leaving out a lot of women, and it needs an explanation to know what it is. Or a name like "Fragrant Offerings" is not going to be meaningful to anyone who hasn't read a decent amount of the Bible. If your goal is outreach, no one from the neighborhood will have any idea what you're about with a name like this.

Keep these things in mind as you name your group. It can be fun to have a name, but be sure it's a name that works *for* you instead of *against* you.

Here are a few tips to keep in mind:

- If you use an acrostic, be sure you (and everyone else) can remember what it stands for.

- Uncommon words from the Bible (like Agape Girls or Koinonia Club) might have an awesome meaning...but if they're hard to say or spell or the average woman who goes to your church won't have any idea what that word means, it will be a turnoff and might actually discourage women from coming.

- Words that are trendy may go out of style within a year. Will the name be relevant in two years?

- Avoid words that are associated only with a certain age group or demographic. You want your ministry to be inclusive of all women— not just those over 50 or only those who are married, and so on.

- Invite several women from different age groups to share their ideas before you finalize anything.

Ideas we have for names:

Building A TEAM

Even Jesus worked with others, so ministry as a team is definitely important! Just as ministries differ across churches, teams will differ as well. We've provided some tips to help you build a healthy team, including how to invite people to join your team, how to assess your strengths as a team, and how to grow stronger together.

We're also including ideas on different ministry roles you might have within your team—but keep in mind, most women's ministries are small and most churches only have two to five women on their team. Some function just fine with one person taking the lead and everyone else jumping in as needed. Other teams like to have specific roles for each person to cover all the bases and make sure no one is spread too thin. As you move through this section and pray with those on your team, you'll be able to decide which approach is best for your ministry.

Prepare to Invite Others

Getting women to join our teams can be a challenge, and while we don't want to say there are "wrong" ways to grow your team, there definitely are right ways! The very best way is to personally talk to someone, whether in person or on the phone, but not through a mass email or through an announcement in the church bulletin. You'll include three elements in your conversation:

• Affirm

• Invite

• Share your personal experience

This should take about 90 seconds, and it should be done in person. For example:

"Melissa, I notice how friendly you are to everyone, and people are naturally drawn to you. I think you'd be a perfect fit as a greeter, welcoming women as they arrive to Bible study each week. I have made so many friends since I joined the women's team, and I believe this is how God is using me to make a difference."

See that this starts with **affirmation**. You affirm the person with something specific you've noticed about her—so you actually have to pay attention to people around you.

Next, you **invite** her to join your team. Ideally you would invite her to take a specific role, such as Bible study leader, greeter, retreat director, and so on. But at the beginning of this process, you may not even know what roles you need, so it's okay to say, "I'd like to invite you to join our team. We're just getting started, so there are a lot of options to consider. But you won't have to do everything alone. That's why we're putting together at team!"

Finally, **share a bit** about how this has been meaningful in your own life—so she hears your own passion for ministry. Even if you haven't started yet, you can share what your dream is by telling her the mission statement. (It's already coming in handy!)

It's short and sweet—and works! For best results, write a few sample invitations here so you've got this in mind the next time you're ready to use it!

 **My invitation message:**

Look for Women to Invite

Prayer is your starting point here. Ask God to open your eyes to women around you who might be a good fit for your team. It's likely there are women all around you who would love to be involved if they were personally invited by you, so first ask God to give you ideas.

Here are women God has brought to mind:

_____

_____

_____

_____

_____

> "He makes the whole body fit together perfectly. As each part does its own special work, it helps the other parts grow, so that the whole body is healthy and growing and full of love."
>
> —Ephesians 4:16

Even if you don't have a structured women's ministry in place, you likely have women who have been serving other women in some way—planning an annual retreat, leading Bible studies, coordinating baby showers. These would be logical women to include in your invitation as well. You can also ask church leaders for ideas of people whom God has brought to their attention.

Most of the time, putting an announcement in a church bulletin gets very little results. But you may want to put a brief announcement in stating that anyone who is interested can connect with you for more information (and be sure to put your contact info with that!). Then you can have coffee with those interested and see if they share your passion for ministry.

What I'm Inviting People to Do

Keep in mind, the list below is a guideline. And if you're just getting started, you don't even know what roles you have need of. Use these roles as they work for your ministry. It is not essential you have someone for each of these (in reality, most churches only have a few people on their team!). You'll also discover more about people you'll want to join your team as you move through the next section.

> "Two people are better off than one, for they can help each other succeed. If one person falls, the other can reach out and help. But someone who falls alone is in real trouble. Likewise, two people lying close together can keep each other warm. But how can one be warm alone? A person standing alone can be attacked and defeated, but two can stand back-to-back and conquer. Three are even better, for a triple-braided cord is not easily broken."
>
> —Ecclesiastes 4:9-12

• Leadership Coordinator

The Leadership Coordinator oversees the women's ministry team and encourages leadership development. She oversees the women's ministry but is not responsible for *doing* everything (that's why you build a team!). You're also creating ministry opportunities *for* women.

• Prayer Team Coordinator

We suggest designating a woman to coordinate prayer for your ministry and the women you'll touch. She'll notify others as urgent prayer needs arise and coordinate others to pray.

• Events Coordinator

This person oversees events and retreats. These typically involve a lot of logistics (where to meet, budgeting, making sure food is ready, and so on). Invite someone who is good with details to take this role.

- **Publicity Coordinator**

  Who loves to talk and spread the word about events, groups, and more? This is your Publicity Coordinator! She'll oversee spreading the word throughout your church and community about what you're doing.

- **Growth Groups Coordinator**

  This coordinator makes sure Bible studies are available for women of all ages and life stages. Perhaps you already offer a Bible study once or twice a week at your church or have a variety of smaller groups meeting in homes. If you have them going, keep up the good work!

- **Connection Groups Coordinator**

  Many churches form shared-interest groups that help women connect and build friendships based on common interests and passions. These are different than Bible study groups. Women who have hesitations about getting involved in a Bible study—either because they feel intimidated, aren't ready spiritually, or they've been wounded by past experiences—are often more likely to try a shared-interest group. And women who are involved in Bible studies often still want opportunities to casually connect with others.

  Women who like scrapbooking might become Sassy Scrappers. Women who enjoy reading and discussing books might become Lit 'n' Lattes. Your church might have Where Moms Connect in order to encourage moms. The Connection Groups Coordinator is designated to keep in contact with the leaders of each of these groups, providing encouragement and helping coordinate dates and space usage as well as cross-promoting each other's groups, events, and fundraisers.

Here's what my team looks like now:

_____

_____

_____

_____

_____

Here's my dream team (the team I'm praying for!):

_____

_____

_____

_____

_____

_____

DESIGNING YOUR WOMEN'S MINISTRY

MAKING A Design Plan

At this point you should have a mission statement and at least one or two other women on your team. It's time to make a design plan for your ministry! (This is where it really starts to get fun!) Go through this process with your team.

Step One

Make a list of everything *currently available* for women in your church. Avoid discussing your likes and dislikes. On your list include Bible studies, events, service opportunities, retreats, and so on.

This is what we currently have available for women:

_____

_____

_____

Step Two

Create a Design Wheel based on your mission statement. You'll find several different design wheels on the following pages—choose the one that has the right number of "slices" for your mission statement. For example, if your mission statement is "To connect women with God, connect women with others, and connect others with God," you'll use the design wheel with three sections. In one you'll write "connect women with God," in the next you'll write "connect women with others," and in the last you'll write "connect others with God."

You'll find design wheels that have two, three, four, and five sections on the following pages. If your mission statement has more than 5 parts to it, we suggest you revisit your statement as you likely are trying to do too much!

Once you've chosen the wheel that works with your mission statement and written your focus areas on the wheel, turn to the pages after the wheels and find out what to do next.

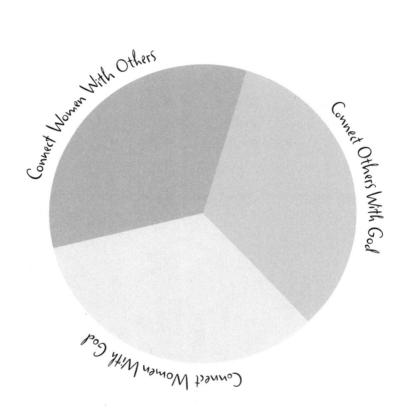

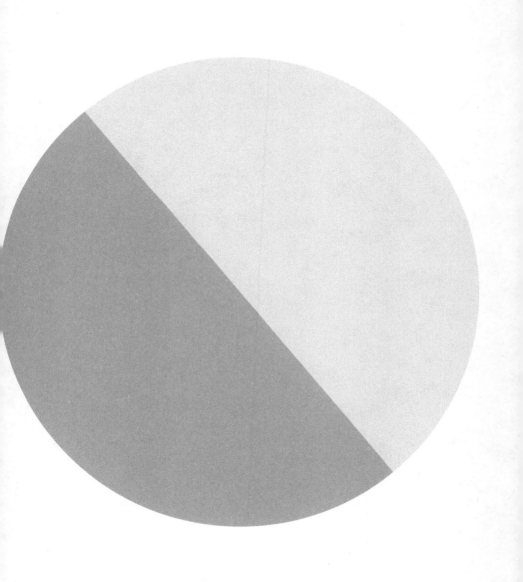

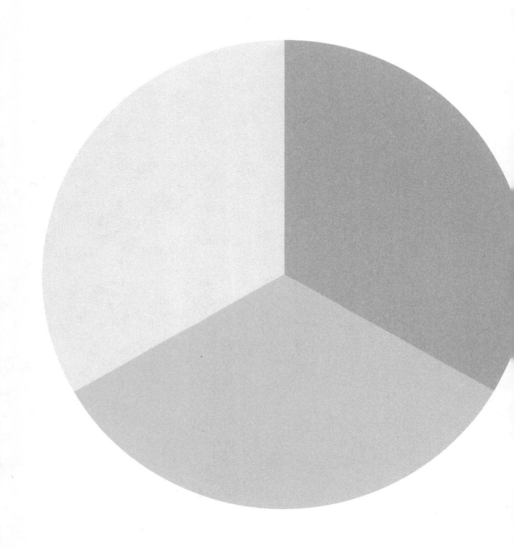

DESIGNING YOUR WOMEN'S MINISTRY

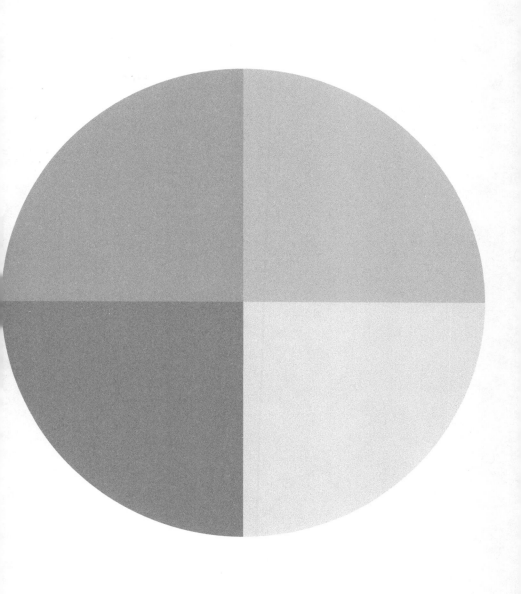

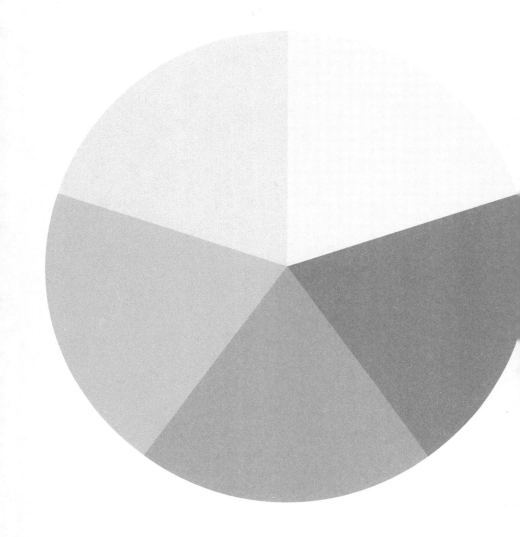

DESIGNING YOUR WOMEN'S MINISTRY

Step Three

Transfer each item from the list you created in Step One to the design wheel under the category in which it fits. For example, if you host a summer picnic that helps women get to know each other, put "summer picnic" in the "connect women with others" section of your design wheel. Bible studies would go in the "connect women with God" section, and so on. You'll find that this step will lead to a good amount of discussion, as there are some activities that don't fit neatly into one category. For example, a retreat might help women connect with others and with God. You can discuss this together to see what your team thinks is the key reason for having retreats, and then put this activity into that category—or you may allow yourselves a bit of leeway and write retreats across two sections. It's up to you.

You may notice you have items on your list from Step One which don't seem to fit in any of the categories. If you have a few of those, write them outside the design wheel.

The goal of this step is to ensure that what you're offering for women is both balanced and matches with your mission statement. For example, if you plan too many outreach events or study opportunities, your wheel will be out of balance and women will have difficulty experiencing the full purpose of your ministry. It doesn't mean the outreach events or study opportunities should be eliminated, but you'll need to consider how these balance with your entire ministry. If you have a "flat tire" in ministry, your women will not thrive and grow.

And if you have activities and events that don't fit with the mission you've stated, you're going to have trouble keeping focus within your team and your ministry. The next step will help you get on track!

Step Four

In this step you'll "SACK" your current ministry! This is going to lead to a lot of discussion, which is great! You're really going to know your focus after you get through this step.

Move through these four "SACK" sections together. Discuss each one respectfully and without any eye-rolling. ☺ Keep in mind the balance of your design wheel. Are you currently "flat" in any area? Are you overloaded in any area? Refer to your design wheel throughout this process.

Stop. What should we stop doing? Old programs are sometimes kept alive only because "we've always done them." Even the best ministries can become dated and no longer effective. You can stop the program or change it, considering how it fits in your purpose wheel. (Any items from Step One that didn't make it onto your design wheel might be candidates for "Stop.")

Our Stop list:

_____

_____

_____

_____

_____

_____

RESPECT IN TRANSITIONS

When you stop something, acknowledge the women who have served in the past, assuring them of their worthwhile service and inviting them to continue to use their gifts and talents in new and refreshing ways.

Whether you decide to keep, add, or stop something in your women's ministry, remember to honor those who serve. While you may not personally understand or appreciate every approach to ministry, consider that at the heart of ministry is a passion for reaching women. Regardless of the approach, we share the same passion. And we can stand together on common ground regardless of differences.

Add. Which of the sections of your purpose wheel are blank or underdeveloped? Plan to add what's needed in your ministry. Remember, you won't make all these changes at once, but begin to dream and make plans. You don't have to know exactly what you'll add at this moment; simply note that you need to add. For example, you may see that you don't have any outreach going on, but one of your mission statement sections calls for outreach. In the "Add" area you might write "Add outreach!" and come back to this later to plan what the exact outreach will look like. But you'll know this needs to be done.

Our Add list:

_____

_____

_____

_____

Change. Perhaps you need to make some updates. Use smaller strategic teams to implement changes. Perhaps you have Bible studies, but you realize you need to offer a wider variety or try a new approach. Perhaps you have an annual event, but you realize the same women attend every year, and you want to include women of various ages as well as women throughout the community. Whether you're adding something new or tweaking events and groups you already have in place, realize you don't need to do all the research and creating. We're here to help. We'll encourage and equip you in every step of ministry!

Our Change list:

_____

_____

_____

_____

Keep. It works! Keep it.

Our Keep list:

_____

_____

_____

_____

Intentionally plan and evaluate in this way at least once a year. Listen to your team and maximize the resources available to you.

Thriving Through Change

Going through the design wheel exercise likely has brought up the issue of change. Some things need to stop. Some things need to start. Some things need to change. And change is hard! Many of us will admit things aren't working great, but making steps to change can hurt feelings, feel risky, and simply be frustrating.

Change is inevitable. But you can take steps to prepare for the changes that will come to your women's ministry. Women may leave or shift leadership roles, new women will join the team, priorities and budgets may change, and ideas may be added or discarded. That's why it's important to learn about the nature of change and how it can affect your ministry.

INCLUDE EVERYONE IN THE CHANGE PROCESS

When we make changes for others without including them, we set ourselves up for confrontations, hurt feelings, and frustration. Engage the entire team in the process of preparing for and transitioning through change, and everyone will be able to handle it better. Make team decisions, not "I'm the queen" decisions.

THE BEST TIME TO CHANGE IS BEFORE YOU HAVE TO

A living, growing ministry will never stay the same—to stay alive it *needs* to change! Since change is inevitable and we prefer to be agents of change instead of reactors to change, plan ahead and anticipate the changes that need to happen to best grow your women.

CHANGE MAKES PEOPLE FEEL INSECURE

It's easy to get comfortable with the way things are done or with the people who do them. Often we get a sense of security from our surroundings. But our security can't be dependent on what's happening on the outside. The only real security comes from a strong trust in God and strong bonds of trust with our ministry partners. Taking everything to God in prayer, both alone and with the team, will help you stand on a solid rock of trust when the winds of change start to blow.

THERE ARE DIFFERENT KINDS OF CHANGE

Many changes happen continuously over time. God has us in a continual process of change to be more like Christ. The same is true of our ministries. God's continually helping and guiding us to be better and better at reaching women for Jesus!

But sometimes an abrupt change will happen. A leader leaves, a key helper moves, or a new person joins the team. Maybe a catastrophic or tragic event happens in your community and you're called to respond. How do we prepare for both kinds of change? Read the Bible, pray, and develop strong and supportive relationships with other women. Develop an attitude of gratitude, a strong faith, and friends you can count on!

PEOPLE REACT TO CHANGE IN DIFFERENT WAYS

- **Moving Forward.** These people are supportive of change and keep the future in mind in planning for change. When change happens, they look for ways to make the change work. They assess their feelings about the change and take a personal responsibility to support change for a positive outcome.

- **Neutral.** These people "go along" with changes but don't commit themselves to supporting them. They may be indecisive or have other reasons for withholding support. They may complain about changes but don't actively work for or against them.

- **Moving Against.** These are people who tend to place blame and point fingers in reaction to change. They can be vocal and visible or passive and covert. People who disagree with changes sometimes want things to fail in order to be proven "right." They might even sabotage efforts for change.

GREAT LEADERS WELCOME CHANGE

In fact, they love it! Why? Because they thrive on challenge and love problem-solving for positive change. They're also adaptable and can stand on this promise of Scripture:

And we know that God causes everything to work together for the good of those who love God and are called according to his purpose for them.

(Romans 8:28)

There are leaders who develop followers and leaders who develop leaders. Jesus had followers, but he invested most of his time in developing leaders who could carry on the ministry after he was gone. Which leads us right into our next section!

DESIGNED TO WORK AS A Team

If you were to redecorate your living room, what kind of patterns would you choose? Vibrant stripes? A room packed with polka dots? One color with no variation at all? Can you imagine if you had one (and only one) choice and had to stick with that forever? How boring! It's nice to have a variety of options.

Take a look at the people around you. God loves variety, too! And it's through that variety that we can join with others and create teams that get to work to get things done in many different ways.

We've created an assessment to help you get to know whom God made you to be and how you can work better with the women you work and serve with. When we better understand who we are (not who we *think* we are but who God made us to be)—and who other people are—we can grow, work, and serve together more effectively for God!

Since each person on your team should have her own copy of this book, go ahead and circle your answers to the questions below. Then work through the pages that follow to discover more on how you can best work together as a team.

What's Your Personality Design?

Circle the statement that best describes you in each situation:

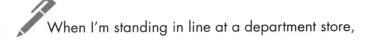

When I'm standing in line at a department store,

A. I want to take charge and get everyone through the checkout line quickly.

B. I chat with people around me while waiting.

C. I allow a person with fewer items to go ahead of me.

D. I quietly wait my turn.

At the beginning of a week,

A. I make a "to-do" list, but I'm flexible in deciding when to work on each task.

B. I'm ready to "wing it" and take each day as it comes.

C. I know what needs to be done, but I'll change my plans if friends or family members have needs.

D. I make a "to-do" list, write a schedule, and I stick to it.

When I play a game with friends,

    A. I decide what game we play and who is on what team.

    B. I try to make sure everyone gets involved in playing.

    C. I prefer playing noncompetitive games.

    D. I ensure we follow the rules.

When choosing what movie to see with friends,

    A. I like to spend as little time as possible in selecting the movie.

    B. I let everyone know what I want to see, but I want everyone to be happy.

    C. I listen to what everyone else wants to see and then go along with the majority.

    D. I figure out the best movie to see based on details like schedule, cost, and content.

When a friend has a problem,

    A. I try to listen, but I want to jump in and fix it!

    B. I listen and talk through some solutions.

    C. I listen and am sympathetic. I'll only offer my opinion if asked.

    D. I want to have time to analyze the problem and consider the best solution.

When planning an event,

   A. I take charge and make sure everything is done.

   B. I make sure everyone is involved and doing what they enjoy.

   C. I get involved where my friends are involved.

   D. I work behind the scenes, taking care of details.

When changing a tradition, I say,

   A. "It's about time!"

   B. "Let's consider all the pros and cons."

   C. "How does everyone else feel about it?"

   D. "Why change? Things are fine the way they are!"

When starting a new project,

   A. I get excited if it involves worthwhile and challenging goals.

   B. I love to discuss it with all my friends.

   C. I don't like new projects unless my friends are involved.

   D. I focus on gathering the facts.

If I'm honest about my friendships,

    A. I get to know people very easily, but I don't allow many to get too close.

    B. I have tons of friends and am usually the ringleader when hanging out.

    C. I have many friends, and I like to get to know each one well.

    D. I invest deeply in just a few friends.

When I experience conflict,

    A. I confront it and move on to other things.

    B. I help fix it because I want everyone to get along.

    C. I avoid it because I want everyone to get along.

    D. I analyze it and look for the most logical way to deal with it.

When I consider rearranging the furniture in my house,

    A. I imagine how I want it to look and rearrange furniture once.

    B. I move furniture often, because I like variety.

    C. I'll ask my friends for advice.

    D. I prefer to keep it where it is unless there is a good reason to move it.

When I travel,

    A. I like to make plans in advance and then stick to the schedule.

    B. I enjoy new experiences and can take off and explore with few plans.

    C. I want to be with people I know and do things everyone enjoys.

    D. I like to visit familiar places and prefer to stay near home.

When I organize my house,

    A. I have a practical place for everything, but I'll rearrange as needed.

    B. I don't take the time for much organization.

    C. I keep most things where I've always kept them.

    D. I like to have a place for everything and everything kept in its place.

When I'm shopping for a new outfit,

    A. I know exactly what I want and don't like to settle for anything else.

    B. I have an idea of what I want, but I find other things I like while shopping.

    C. I usually buy specific types of clothes at my usual stores.

    D. I compare several outfits in several stores before deciding on the best deal.

If I start a new exercise routine,

    A. I have a plan with short- and long-term goals, but I make adjustments as needed.

    B. I start off optimistically but might not finish.

    C. I prefer to have girlfriends join with me.

    D. I have a plan with short- and long-term goals, and I'm determined to meet all goals.

If I see someone sitting by herself at a women's event,

    A. I find someone who can connect with her.

    B. I get her involved by having her join me in fun activities.

    C. I sit next to her and try to start a conversation.

    D. I'm generally too hesitant to approach her.

When a girlfriend has a crisis,

    A. I fix it.

    B. I help her fix it.

    C. I listen.

    D. I ask her for facts.

When friends are coming to my house,

   A. I plan ahead and have almost everything done before friends arrive, but I give them a task if they offer to help.

   B. I plan only as much as necessary and then have friends help as they arrive.

   C. I plan based on what I know my friends enjoy, and I let them help if they would like to be involved.

   D. I plan all details ahead of time and want everything to be done before friends arrive.

When I am upset,

   A. I spend a little time on my own and then move on to other things.

   B. I get together with a group of girlfriends.

   C. I call one of my closest friends.

   D. I spend time on my own and try to figure out the best solution.

When talking on the phone,

    A. I take care of business.

    B. I have long, fun, meandering conversations.

    C. I have conversations based on what's going on in my friends' lives.

    D. I prefer not to talk on the phone except to ask or answer simple questions.

When I first meet someone,

    A. I'm excited about getting to know someone new, but I won't share much right away.

    B. I jump right in and find out all I can about her.

    C. I take my time getting to know her, and I enjoy listening to her.

    D. I want to get to know her before deciding if we're going to be good friends.

After a busy week,

    A. I might briefly relax but then begin to plan for the next week.

    B. I want to have some fun with a group of friends.

    C. I choose one or two close friends to hang out with.

    D. I will relax if I have time, but I will often do other things on my "to-do" list.

When I hear a girlfriend is upset with me,

    A. I contact her and work it out.

    B. I find out from other friends what's going on, then decide if I should contact her.

    C. I hesitate to contact her and just hope the problem will go away.

    D. I gather facts for a long time to try to decide if I should contact her.

If a girlfriend asks my opinion,

    A. I tell her what I think (even without being asked)!

    B. I give it, but I'll be encouraging no matter what the situation.

    C. I hesitate to share, because I want to hear what she thinks.

    D. I share only if I have enough facts to have formed an opinion.

Now total the number of each letter you circled:

    A. _____

    B. _____

    C. _____

    D. _____

What Does It All Mean?

A= CHEVRON

Bold, sharp, and with a bit of zigzag added, Chevron Personalities thrive under pressure. They make decisions quickly and easily and are often in leadership positions. They are always on the go and marking items off the "to-do" list, keeping the big picture in view. Chevrons get bored when life isn't changing or seems too frivolous. They embrace change, especially when they are the change agents. Because Chevrons typically do not shy away from confrontation, they often seem harsh. They don't always take time to listen. Chevrons have a lot of acquaintances but have few close friends.

B= POLKA DOTS

Where there are polka dots, there are often women; and where there are Polka Dot Personalities, there are usually more girlfriends! Polka Dot Personalities are women who love to talk and don't like to be alone. They connect well with lots of women and encourage everyone to get involved. Polka Dots are usually in the middle of large groups… the drama queens! They often focus on the social aspect of teamwork and avoid details. Polka Dots jump into a conflict quickly without considering all the consequences. They want to fix things and help everyone feel better. Polka Dots make great emcees at events. They also rally teams and have a lot of friends.

C= PLAID

Plaid is a beautiful mix of colors and is especially fun when it's on flannel pajamas. Plaid Personalities are the ones you want around for comfort. They love people and are willing to listen as well as share, taking time to invest in girlfriends' lives. But while they soak in the comfort of friends, they avoid the conflict that comes with friends. They want everyone to be happy. Plaid personalities are dependable and committed, so they'll only accept change over time. These women are great at involving people, but detailed tasks will usually suffer.

D= SOLID

Solid Personalities are just that—dependable, structured, and "no nonsense." They stay on task and will try to keep everyone else in a group organized and on task as well. Solids want to cross all the t's and dot all the i's, and they thrive when in roles that primarily involve tasks rather than people. They can be seen as picky or judgmental when trying to keep everyone on task because they have difficulty separating tasks and people when working on a problem or plan. Solids are hesitant to change and will only do so once a situation has been thoroughly analyzed. These women typically have a select few trusted friends.

Here's my Personality Design:

_____

_____

_____

_____

Share your personality styles. Refrain from commenting on each other's styles at this point. Write team members' names next to the personality styles to refer to later.

Personality Designs of others on our team:

_____

_____

_____

_____

Here's a list of some qualities of each of the personality styles. Take a look at your primary personality style and **circle** the quality you think is your best strength. Put a **line** through the quality you think is your biggest weakness.

Chevron	Polka Dot	Plaid	Solid
Take charge	Fast-paced	Listener	Perceptive
Change-agent	Talkative	Dependable	Reliable
Confrontational	Social	Cautious of change	Precise
Determined	Encouraging	Investor	Organized
Leader	Fixer	Avoid conflict	Hesitant to change
Confident	Optimistic	Comforter	Analyzer
Assertive	Avoid details	Patient	Task-focused
Big-picture focus	Accept change	Consistent	Intentional
Decisive	Energetic	Downplay details	Practical
Persistent	Creative	Supporter	Avoid conflict

Note that no one Design is better than another. God made us different on purpose! Knowing how each of us functions best can help us know where we're strong as a team, and it also helps us know where we'll need to give each other grace. For example...

> "He makes the whole body fit together perfectly. As each part does its own special work, it helps the other parts grow, so that the whole body is healthy and growing and full of love."
>
> —Ephesians 4:16

During social time...

- Chevrons want to take "social time" off the list of things to do.
- Polka Dots want to talk...and talk and talk.
- Plaids want to relax and enjoy being around friends.
- Solids are overwhelmed by all the commotion.

When working on specific tasks...

- Chevrons want to be sure everyone is being productive.
- Polka Dots want to be sure everyone is involved.
- Plaids want to be sure everyone is happy.
- Solids want to be sure all details are checked off the "to-do" list.

When working with a deadline...

- Chevrons make sure the job gets done whatever it takes.
- Polka Dots involve as many people as possible and have little concern for the deadline.
- Plaids "keep the peace" through any moments of tension.
- Solids make lists and will only feel the job is done when all tasks are checked off the list.

When serving on a team together…

- Chevrons will keep the big picture in view but will frustrate Polka Dots and Plaids by not allowing enough social time.

- Polka Dots will involve many women but will frustrate Chevrons with too much social chat and Solids with too little attention to detail.

- Plaids will keep peace among a team but will frustrate Chevrons and Polka Dots with resistance to change and Solids with time spent listening to people instead of working on tasks.

- Solids will ensure that everything gets done but will frustrate Chevrons and Polka Dots for not working quickly enough and Plaids for not listening to everyone's opinions.

Discuss:

- In what circumstance can your strength become a weakness?
- In what circumstance will your weakness become a strength?

The Perfect Blend

Despite the conflicts, groups of women are stronger when different personalities work together. We acknowledge our weaknesses and use our strengths. We try to understand each other and encourage everyone to serve where they fit best. And as we learn about the women we serve with, perhaps the best thing we can do for our teams is to understand ourselves better.

There are ways to use your strengths and your team's strengths to work through conflicts, but you have to…

- Look at the big picture…which is a Chevron trait.
- Connect with each other…which is a Polka Dot trait.
- Listen compassionately to each other…which is a Plaid trait.
- Keep focused…which is a Solid trait.

You need the balance. You need every personality!

> "I want them to be encouraged and knit together by strong ties of love. I want them to have complete confidence that they understand God's mysterious plan, which is Christ himself."
>
> —Colossians 2:2

Want More?

Another great way to develop your team is to learn what your spiritual gifts are and share those as a team. This might also help each person be affirmed as to how she is best equipped by God to serve in ministry and helps the whole team discover how they fit together in God's plan.

We recommend an online tool called Spiritual Gifts Discovery. For one flat rate, your entire church will have unlimited access to this site and the assessments, which can be done in print form, online, or on mobile devices. For more information, go to group.com/adult-ministry/spiritual-gifts-discovery.

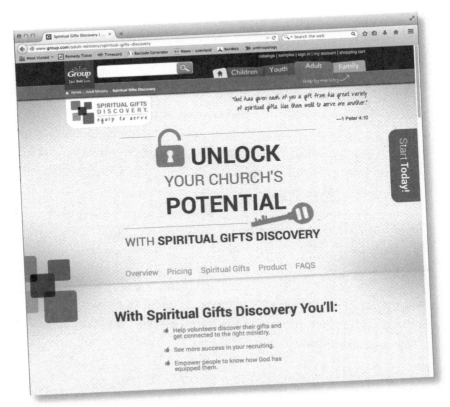

AN ENERGY-EFFICIENT Design

Some homes and appliances are designed to save energy—and really, who doesn't want to save energy? Our teams can work together in energy-efficient ways as well, which means you'll use your time wisely and avoid burnout. This section will help you with that!

Meaningful Meetings

One challenge many of us face is the use of our time. And many meetings end up being big time-wasters. We need to value the busy lives of our team members. We have a responsibility to organize and plan meetings that accomplish our goals yet also build community and keep women fired up for friendships, fun, and faith! Planning and running a successful meeting is one way to avoid burnout and a great way to keep your leadership team vibrant. Here's how.

CREATE A COMPELLING REASON

Don't promote your team meetings as "just another leadership meeting." Create a compelling reason—a "can't miss" experience—that keeps women excited to attend. Brainstorm with your team for ideas that inspire them. You might offer free massages 15 minutes before the meeting, begin with a prayer walk around the perimeter of your church, or delegate responsibility for parts of the meeting to different team members. Women will develop a sense of ownership when you allow them to help create the compelling reasons for your meetings.

Go ahead and brainstorm together now, listing a few ideas that might make meetings more "can't miss." Make sure these are actually do-able ideas (so having a chef show up each time you meet with a gourmet meal prepared is likely not do-able, but starting with a prayer walk or with a sundae bar might be easy to implement). You don't have to have something like this at every meeting, but you'll want to include these often so no one wants to miss out!

Our ideas:

_____

_____

_____

_____

SCHEDULE FOR SUCCESS

If women are consistently late for your meetings, consider whether the meeting time or date needs to change. To help women arrive on time, consider choosing a unique starting time and find a verse or theme to match. For example, a meeting that starts at 6:33 could be paired with Matthew 6:33: "Seek the Kingdom of God above all else, and live righteously, and he will give you everything you need." Or design a meeting with an airplane motif and start at 7:47!

Talk about times that do—and don't—work for your team. Make notes here about that conversation, knowing that these may change as life changes!

_____

_____

_____

_____

STAY ON TIME

Commit to starting your meetings on time, even if everyone is not there. This conveys respect for women's busy schedules and honors those who come on time. Start when you say you'll start and stop when you say you'll stop.

HAVE AN AGENDA (A REAL ONE, NOT THE ONE IN YOUR HEAD)

Send an agenda to your team before the meeting so they have time to think about the topics. Allow team members to be involved in setting the meeting agenda. This can easily be emailed to everyone the day before the meeting. And if anyone has items to add, they can let the agenda-setter know promptly. Structure your meetings so the "must cover" issues are completed at least 15 minutes before the end of your meeting.

NO POP QUIZZES

Let your team know ahead of time what questions you'll be asking and the issues you'll need their feedback on during your meeting. They'll be able to share out of reflection rather than reaction.

MINIMIZE INFORMATION OVERLOAD

Use email or printed handouts to share calendars, facts, and details that everyone needs to know. Save your meeting times for focusing on the things you need to be *together* to accomplish.

BUILD COMMUNITY

Women have two primary motivations for involvement in women's ministry: to spend time with women and to serve God. If you don't create a sense of community and value fun interaction, your team members may find reasons why they can't attend a team meeting. So be sure you play, pray, and prosper together!

What are a few ideas for fun things your team can do together? Brainstorm together and jot your ideas here:

_____

_____

_____

COMMUNICATE VALUE

Let your team members know how excited you are to see them at meetings. If they're absent, send a friendly note or email to let them know they were missed. And everyone on the team can participate in this, not just the leader!

Be sure to celebrate and honor your volunteers and schedule time to just have fun together. Remember, the team that prays and plays together, stays together!

Getting Away Together

A great way to help your team feel valued, grow women closer as a team, and avoid overload burnout is to plan a getaway just for leaders. If you can work this into your church budget so your volunteers who commit so much time don't have to pay for it, you'll reap huge rewards! Here are a few ideas:

- Take your leadership team on an overnight retreat. Use some of the time for fun and some of the time for big-picture planning. There's nothing like getting away for a full day or an overnight trip to help a team bond, laugh, and make big plans!

- The next time you host a retreat, have your leaders go up one day early—or at least 5 hours early. Arriving early gives everyone a chance to "gel" as a team, share a meal together, and make sure everyone's up to date on the latest retreat agenda.

- Have an afternoon or evening of pampering. Going together for pedicures and then out for dessert is a simple way to share time together and know you're valued. And when word of this spreads, you're likely to have a few new volunteers for the team!

- Identify leaders to others. Have fun and fresh sweatshirts (the kind that zip up the front) made for your leaders and encourage them to wear them to events and gatherings. Others will know who leaders are, and your team will feel special!

Avoid Overloading the Circuits

In any type of ministry, there's always the threat of burnout. Sometimes this happens because of our situation, but often it happens because of choices we make and the expectations we place on others.

The first step to avoiding the dreaded burnout is to identify the challenges that are likely to raise your stress levels. We've gathered a list we commonly hear from women's ministry leaders. Perhaps you and your leadership team have a few to add:

- Managing changes.
- Keeping up with technology.
- Maintaining balance.
- Competing sources for quick answers and solutions.
- Identifying and serving changing needs.
- Building significant relationships.
- Establishing communities as people move.

More we would add to this list:

So how can we meet the challenges of ministry in fast-pasted society? Keep reading!

Cool Down!

As leaders, you keep the ministry passion ignited in your team. But you also need to manage and organize the environment so it's a safe place for women—a place where there's low risk of being burned and hurt. Watch for these symptoms in yourselves (and in the women you're reaching):

- Woundedness: "I feel hurt."
- Frustration: "I can't do it all!" or "Why don't they do more?"
- Immobilization: "I don't know what I should do anymore!"
- Deflated self-esteem: "I'm not good enough."
- Detachment from the purpose: "I can't get excited about it anymore."

You might recognize some of these feelings in a team member or yourself. They're usually the result of operating in an environment that can be hazardous to your ministry and potentially hurt your team members. It's hard to confront the causes, but ignoring these symptoms won't make them go away. So let's talk about it!

If you're experiencing burnout or are on the fringe of it…

- **Pray** about the situation, the people involved, your attitude, and what God would have you learn and do. Don't take this step lightly!

- Ask someone who knows you well for **advice**. Be sure you ask someone who is credible, mature, and healthy in her thinking. This isn't a time for gossip, but a time for seeking counsel.

- Be **honest** with yourself and those around you about your feelings, but refrain from "dumping" with no resolution. Focus on solutions, not problems.

- Take **responsibility** for your part. Did you overcommit? Let others down? Avoid confrontation? Cause an unhealthy confrontation? Not ask for clear directions or enough support?

- Stick to the real issues and seek **resolution** and reconciliation. Whom do you need to talk to in order to work toward solutions? Whom are you upset with (or who is upset with you) that you need to reconcile with?

- Assess the **environment** your team operates in, and identify elements you can help improve. What's working? What's not working? What symptoms of burnout are you and others experiencing?

- **Honor God** in all ways. Allow God to be your leader and direct your thoughts, actions, and words in ways that will bring *him* the honor—not you.

Talk about it. What are you doing to keep cool and avoid burnout? Where do you see signs already? Share with each other and take time now to pray for each other and discuss how you can support each other in avoiding burnout.

> "Don't just pretend to love others. Really love them. Hate what is wrong. Hold tightly to what is good. Love each other with genuine affection, and take delight in honoring each other. Never be lazy, but work hard and serve the Lord enthusiastically."
>
> —Romans 12:9-11

Hi! We're just putting a note in here to say great job! Your team has been working together to lay a sturdy foundation through creating a mission, praying, building a team, and discovering how to be effective in working together and caring for each other.

This next section of the book focuses on implementing your ministry. We'll discover more about reaching the women in your church and community, what's relevant in Bible studies, why and how to host events and special gatherings, and more!

As you move through these sections, keep your Design Wheel in mind. Just because we've given you ideas here doesn't mean you have to do them all. Choose what works best with your mission statement. Work as a team to talk through what you'll offer and why. And always remember you don't have to do everything at once. When you do remodeling on a home, you start with one room and then move to the next one. It's the same with ministry—start with one area and work to make that strong. Then move to the next thing. We're praying for you!

OPEN House!

Share Your New Design With a Kickoff Event!

How will women know what exciting changes you're making? How can you avoid the rumor mill generating discontent about changes? Invite all women to have fun at a kickoff event. Choose a fresh theme you've never tried before. Add scrumptious finger foods, colorful decorations, and stations for women to explore and connect based on their needs and interests.

During this gathering, share what's ahead and let women know how they can get involved. Introduce your team. Tell the new mission statement. Share your passion and enthusiasm by telling your own story. Let women connect with your heart!

Here are a few additional ideas to help you with your kickoff event.

BEFRIEND!

Is welcoming new people and reaching out part of your mission? Be sure everyone is warmly greeted and quickly connected into conversation. One easy way to do this is have women choose a sticker to add to their name tags when they arrive. Offer stickers that relate to the theme of your gathering and are funny or silly. About 15 minutes into your gathering, have women find anyone else with the matching sticker. In these small groups they can share their names and basic info such as where they live or what they do. Then have everyone answer one fun question that will help them get to know the other people a bit better. This could be as simple as "Share about your hobbies" or "Tell what you did for your last vacation." Allow women as much time as they want to keep chatting.

Simple activities like this help women meet others and step outside their existing friendships a bit. It makes it easy for a newcomer to join into a conversation and not feel like an outsider. Never embarrass women in any activity—simply encourage new conversations and ways to find connecting point.

BELONG!

Is helping women connect with others and find a place where they know they belong part of your mission? Expand on the importance of friendships to building community with others.

During your event, have women get into groups of about four to six and brainstorm to discover at least five interests they have in common. When they've done this, have them choose one of those and pretend they're starting a club around that interest. What would they name it? What would they do at their gatherings? Who would join them?

After several minutes, have each group share their ideas with the larger group. Then…see if anyone wants to start one or more of these groups for real! You may end up with a new book club or knitting group or a date on the calendar for women who want to go walking together. Even coming away with one new shared-interest group will be a success!

Emphasize how important it is to provide an opportunity for women to feel like they belong. Mention shared-interest groups, where Christians and those who don't yet know Jesus are able to connect and build relationships.

BELIEVE!

Spiritual growth is likely a part of your ministry purpose. This is an excellent time to let women know what you've got coming ahead or simply to ask them about their interests in the area of Bible study.

If you have a few new studies coming up, have the books and info at

a table at your gathering so women can peruse, ask questions, and see what to expect. Have your sign-up sheet there so women can commit right away.

If you're still gathering ideas, place a few books you're considering on the table and let women tell you which one seems to meet their needs most. Or simply let them write down their own ideas for Bible study (books they like, topics of interest, times of day that work best, and so on) for your leadership team to read through later.

THE BIG PICTURE

Involve others in the decision-making process. Of course, there are large-scale decisions that need to be made by a small team, but when you're planning how to meet the needs of your women, ask them! We've created an interest survey and placed it at the end of this section. You can photocopy this and use it as is, or use this as a guideline to make your own.

Remember to ask women who are already involved in ministry for their input, but also ask those who aren't involved to give their input. It's important to find out why they may not be involved!

BECOME!

It's likely you want to grow your leadership team or help women find ways to use their gifts. Using the interest survey is one way to do this, as well as inviting anyone who is at this gathering to join your next planning meeting. There are so many ways women can serve and make a difference—help them discover where they can plug in and grow into the women God designed them to be!

GETTING TO KNOW *You!*

Name _____

Address _____

Email _____

Phone _____

I'm interested in getting together with other women who enjoy…

☐ Movies   ☐ Cooking

☐ Board Games   ☐ Walking/Exercise

☐ Reading/Discussing   ☐ Crafts

☐ Other: _____

★ Put a star next to any of the above you might be willing to help coordinate.

I'm interested in women's retreats.
Which would you prefer?

☐ One day   ☐ Overnight   ☐ Two nights

What would you like us to include in our retreats?
Check all that apply!

☐ Bible study   ☐ Chat time   ☐ Quiet time

☐ Service project   ☐ Games

☐ Other: _____

  DESIGNING YOUR WOMEN'S MINISTRY

I'm interested in attending these types of Bible studies:

These days/times work best for me:

_____

_____

I'd prefer:

☐ Studies on a book of the Bible

☐ Studies on a topic

☐ Studies with no homework

☐ Studies that include intensive homework

☐ Studies with child care available

☐ Suggested topics: _____

I'm interested in helping with women's ministry.

Area(s) of interest: _____

_____

Do you have additional ideas for our women's ministry? Please share—feel free to write more on the back of this page!

_____

_____

_____

_____

_____

SPREAD THE Word!

Okay. You have some leaders, you have a vision...how will you let others know? How will you get women in your church excited? How will they know what's coming up? What about the community? Are you inviting them too? It's time to start spreading the word!

Remember, the very first place you want to start is with the leaders of your church. Make sure they know your vision, your excitement, and your commitment. Passion and purpose are contagious! Now...how will you promote what's going on? Here's how!

The Basics

There's no way around it. Some of the tried and true methods are still around because they work! Start with those approaches that have worked well in the past for your church. They might include:

- Bulletins
- Media slides (such as PowerPoint or Mediashout)
- Newsletters
- Your church or women's ministry website
- Flyers or brochures

Take advantage of the opportunities you already have at your church. The more exposure you get, the more likely women will be to respond and remember.

Beyond the Basics

After you've considered the "normal" means of communicating, think about one or more of the following ideas. You might be surprised at how willing others will be to help you!

BE INTENTIONAL

Who are you trying to reach? When businesses start a marketing plan, determining target customers is essential and can be time-consuming. But this one is easy for you…you're reaching women! Now, how can you be intentional in finding women to tell about your ministry or to invite to your gatherings?

Brainstorm the "where" and "how" of reaching women in your community. Go where the women are. Parks, coffee shops, spas, fitness centers, daycare centers. How could you reach women in these locations? Whom do you need to ask for permission to post flyers? Who might partner with you in promoting events, or who might even let you have your event in their location?

Watch the traffic flow of women at your church, and promote your ministry where women are. The children's ministry area, coffee and refreshments area, and the women's restrooms. Mirrors and stall doors are great places to share information!

 IT SEEMS SO SIMPLE…

Always include all the essential information in every communication. It surprises us how often the basic info is missing from promotional materials. One church added this to their brochures: "For more information see a women's team member." But they never told who those people were or how to reach them. Don't assume everyone knows the address of the church or the designated entrance, the church's phone number or the coordinator's email address. Provide simple but complete information.

BE A PARTNER

We suggest piggybacking. No, we don't mean you need to jump onto your friend's back! Piggybacking is partnering. For example, if a local hospital is having a health fair, you can offer to host a hospitality area where women can enjoy a healthful drink, a comfortable place to sit and connect, and perhaps a piece of chocolate...dark chocolate, of course. Or if there's a community fair, you can host a pampering area, where women get simple hand massages or fingernail painting. Piggybacking is finding an existing event or other opportunity to partner, so you get to serve others while also providing visibility for your women's ministry.

Who on your team would be willing to do a little research or keep her eyes open for opportunities like this? Write her name here:

_____

_____

_____

_____

BE READY TO SHARE

So, you have a *place* to share...but what are you going to say? When someone asks you about your ministry or your upcoming events, be ready! Here's how to prepare:

- **Write it.** Use a concise statement—perhaps your mission statement—and print it on every brochure, business card, handout, letterhead, or promotional item you create.

- **Share stories.** Gather stories of how your ministry has impacted lives. You never know when you'll have an opportunity to share, and you want to be prepared. Print stories for others to read. Have women share at gatherings. Testimonials powerfully illustrate the success of your ministry!

- **Be visual.** In addition to words, use color, graphics, and visual images to convey the message of your ministry. Take pictures at your events and activities and use them on posters, in brochures, and anywhere else you can to illustrate how your ministry is befriending women and encouraging them to grow into the women God wants them to be!

The Personal Touch

Effective promotions among the church and community often hinge on building *relationships*. Women value relationships, so do what you can to help women connect. When you equip all women to connect with their friends, family, neighbors, and co-workers, you take the responsibility out of your own hands and spread your marketing effectiveness across many women. Your reach is limited. Each time you equip another person to reach additional women, your reach is multiplied.

SIMPLE INVITATIONS

Make it easy for women to invite others. Create fun, simple invitations for women to pick up and share. Make invitations easy to tuck into a greeting card, leave on an office desk, or tuck into a neighbor's front door.

FRIEND DISCOUNTS

Combine women's love for friendships and desire to get great deals by extending friend discounts for events and retreats. If women buy a ticket for themselves, they can purchase as many tickets as they want for their friends for half price (or whatever discount is best for your budget). You might want to be clear you intend for friends to be those who don't regularly attend your church.

EASY REMINDERS

Give women a reminder the final weekend before your event. As women leave worship services, distribute something creative as a reminder. Planning a movie night? Hand out small bags of popcorn with two movie tickets—using the business card template—one to share with a friend. What about a Girls' Night Out with a recycling theme? Print flyers on colored paper and wad the flyers into a (new) trash can. Hand women a piece of trash as they leave the building. Print labels for chocolate bars for a chocolate-themed event.

Influencer Marketing

Who are the "influencers" in your church and community? Get them excited about what you're doing, and they'll be more likely to spread the word with you. This might be as simple as sharing your ministry purpose with church leaders. When you get buy-in from key leaders, they'll share the ministry with others.

Key influencers are also businesses in your community. Invite vendors to partner with you, and you'll both benefit. They may be willing to donate time, services, or products to your events or let you advertize in their businesses with flyers or posters. Allow them to give out business cards or coupons at your event, or mention them in your program brochure to be sure they're thanked appropriately for their part in your event. You'll benefit by promoting your event in community businesses, and the businesses will benefit by exposure at your event.

Think about the people you know in your church and community who own or work at prominent positions in businesses. Consider how each of those people or businesses might be able to help promote your women's ministry. Perhaps you won't be able to tap into each and every business you've listed, but don't limit yourself too quickly. Think outside the box.

We know one women's ministry who partnered with a local bakery. The owner was willing to help promote the ministry by coming up with a special "Girlfriends Cupcake" to sell in her bakery. Each time someone orders the cupcake, the person filling the order places a small card with information about the women's ministry in the bag with the cupcake. The card has basic information on it: church name and address, website, email and phone number, and a friendly invitation to "Check out a place where you'll make friends and find a place to belong."

So many times we run ourselves ragged by our marketing plans. We get stuck in the "take a flyer to every imaginable business" routine, and while flyers are great for some locations and events, think about what impact you can have if you build key relationships with people and businesses and let something they're already doing also help you promote women's ministry!

Key Questions to Ask… Again and Again

Wrestle with questions like these with your leadership team…and just get out there and ask women too! These will help you as you're getting the word out.

- Why do women choose not to get involved?
- What barriers might be keeping women from joining us?
- Why do women start attending groups and events? Why do they stop?
- What follow-up and connection plan is in place for women?

Continue to connect with women who are involved, and ask them what appeals to them and why they continue to stay involved. Ask women who leave through the back door what initially appealed to them and what would have helped them stay involved.

Refrain from relying on assumptions as you evaluate your ministry. Listen to women and share stories. Don't get stuck in the negative opinions, but don't ignore them either. Take an honest look at your ministry on a regular basis (remember the evaluation process!) and be consistent with who God wants you to be.

After reviewing this section, what are the "aha" thoughts that come to mind? Discuss the questions from the section above and jot notes and ideas here:

_____

_____

_____

_____

_____

_____

_____

_____

_____

_____

_____

WE PLANNED...BUT NO ONE CAME!

A challenge that frustrates many leaders is getting women to come to events and gatherings. After you've gone to all the trouble of planning a Bible study, Girls' Night Out, or a retreat, women in your church seem ho-hum about it and don't rush to sign up.

Let's face it. Women are busy. And often what we're offering feels like one more thing to add to an already long list. The key to not being just another "to-do" on a list is to be sure your ministry is connecting. We cannot stress enough how important it is to actually talk to the women you are hoping to reach. This means taking time to personally invite a few women out for coffee once a month to hear what their needs and interests are—or something else that is face to face and involves an actual conversation. Try it. It really works!

DESIGNED FOR RELATIONSHIP With God

Leading women to discover a growing friendship with Jesus is exciting, and it should be the purpose of every women's ministry! Women get to know Jesus as they worship, study, experience, and explore faith together. They get a chance to go deeper and understand why you're reaching out to them in the first place—because of Jesus' love! This section guides you in doing this well and with vibrant results!

Bible Studies

Most churches usually do well at providing Bible studies, but it's important to regularly evaluate what you're offering. Remember, you want to keep your studies fresh and effective. As a team, discuss these questions.

How do the studies we offer vary in format, length, and depth?

How do our studies serve women's varying schedules?

How do our studies reach women with different learning styles?

REACHING MORE WOMEN

As you evaluate and plan, invite others to give input. Get input from a representative sample of women you're trying to reach. If you only ask women already involved in group studies, you might not gain information indicating any changes need to be made. When you ask women *not* involved in current studies, you'll begin to see gaps in what you're offering and can move forward to make some changes... to reach more women and impact their lives for Jesus!

Be sure you're talking to women who are younger than you and older than you, women who are married and those who are not, women with children and those who don't have kids, and so on. Just because something works for you doesn't mean it works for every other woman in your church or community.

As a team, consider who you have not invited into the conversation (meaning personally talking to them face to face instead of making assumptions).

Here are the names of a few women we could get input from:

_____

_____

_____

_____

REFRESH YOUR FORMAT

When a group of women are passionate about studying God's Word and find a format they enjoy, they tend to use that same format over and over. There's nothing wrong with this, but it may leave out others who don't enjoy that format. (Keep the whole "design" analogy in mind—not everyone likes country décor and not everyone likes modern. Different is okay!)

You're reaching women throughout the community, and you want to structure your study groups for a kaleidoscope of women so they can build relationships and grow in their most important relationship... with Jesus.

There are many studies available, and it can be overwhelming to know where to begin. Start by recognizing differences among studies.

- **Length.** Most studies range from 6 to 12 sessions. How often you meet (weekly or every other week) will impact how long the study will last.

- **Leader helps.** Look for studies that offer tips and helpful coaching for leaders. Things like how to moderate when one person talks too much or what to do when someone asks difficult questions.

- **Technology.** Whether a study is DVD-based or is technology-free impacts the experience of the women as well as the choice of the group leader. While watching a DVD is easy for leaders... it's not always the best for women in the groups as they don't get a chance to interact and share their own stories and reflections. This is especially true with younger women who are less interested in hearing a speaker and more interested in relevant, faith-based conversations. Keep the needs of women in mind as you're making your choices.

- **Additional Considerations.** Does the study stand alone, or is it part of a series? What learning styles are targeted? Are the Bible verses included in the text of the study, or will women need to already be familiar with the Bible and how to use it? Details matter when you're reaching women at different places in their spiritual journeys.

We know all these details can make decision-making overwhelming but don't despair! Consider the details as opportunities to reach difference niches of women. And remember, you won't try everything at once. Assess the needs, and meet women where they are.

Take time to talk about these considerations. What light bulbs are going off in your head right now?

CRAZY CALENDARS

Women are busy. We know you can't meet *everyone's* schedule needs. And there are women who use their busy schedules as the excuse for not getting involved in a group. There's not much you can do about that except pray and encourage. But for some, seeing your flexibility in what groups you offer will be just the nudge they need to get started.

Consider offering...

- Both day and evening groups. Women working outside their homes are generally available in the evening. Moms who stay home with children may not want to spend time away from family in the evening, and older women may prefer to be out of the house in daylight hours. Choose various times to meet various needs.

- Both weekly and biweekly groups. Some women want the accountability of meeting together every week. (And when you're focusing on getting young moms involved, sometimes they need that adult interaction time!) Others will hesitate to commit to every week. Start with options women see as manageable.

- Various locations. Meet in the comfort of women's homes...in a park... at a local coffee shop or restaurant...in a school while children are in class. Imagine the possibilities! And you'll reach more women when you meet them where they are.

TEACHING OR LEARNING?

When we think about spreading God's Word among women, are we considering the women who are actually doing the learning, or are we more concerned about the teaching? What's the desired result? That God's Word is *taught* or that God's Word is *learned*?

In their book *The Dirt on Learning*, Thom and Joani Schultz, explain it like this:

What do we mean by learner-based? It's an approach with a clear goal: that learners understand, retain, and apply their learning. The focus is on the learner, not the teacher. Its success is based not on how eloquently the sower casts seeds, but on whether the seeds take root and bear fruit. This shift in perspective is an enormous change for most churches. But the results are stunning—"yielding a hundred, sixty or thirty times what was sown" (Matthew 13:23, NIV).

Let's look at some premises in the learner-based approach.

- **Learners are distinct and unique.** People don't all learn the same way. Some learn primarily through their eyes, others through their ears, others through touch and movement. Some are analytical, others more random and global. Some learn faster than others. Learner-based strategies accommodate all learners.

- **What works for the learners** is far more important than what's most comfortable for their teachers or leaders.

- **Learners help guide the learning process.** They're allowed to make choices, follow their curiosity, and explore what interested them. They're encouraged to make learning relevant to their own lives.

- **Learning occurs best when learners enjoy the process.** They'll learn and retain more when the curriculum brings delight; when friendships and interactions with other learners are encouraged; and when learners feel appreciated, respected, and loved.

- **Education is evaluated on what learners understand, retain, and apply**—not merely on what's taught, the completeness of the curriculum, or the eloquence of the teachers. Learning is effective when it creates learner appetite for more learning and an insatiable desire to share the learning with others.

YOUR CHALLENGE

We're not getting women involved in Bible studies just to pass the time; we're all much too busy for that! We want to make a difference in women's lives. We want women's lives to change because they **experience Jesus** through our ministries—not just hear someone talk about him. We want to change the world for God!

Our challenge to you as you strive for a fresh and intentionally designed women's ministry is to take a hard look at what you're offering for Bible study. Grapple with hard questions, being willing to toss out tradition if that's needed, and being willing to truly offer what will grow women in their relationship with Jesus.

GET R.E.A.L.

These elements are essential for true **learning:**

Relational. Encourage learners to interact with each other, which makes learning more effective and helps build Christian friendships.

Experiential. Learners don't just listen or read—they actually experience the lesson or event. So biblical principles stick with them up to nine times longer!

Applicable. Incorporate life application, because Christians should be both hearers and doers of the Word.

Learner-Based. Different people learn in different ways, so provide a variety of methods to draw people closer to Jesus.

As a team, discuss what you've learned from this section on Bible studies. Is there anything in your current program that needs a redesign? Share your thoughts with each other and consider trying something different—even if it's just a few small changes to help reach more women and be more effective in drawing women closer to God.

Notes from our discussion:

_____

_____

_____

_____

_____

_____

Retreats

After Bible studies, most women's ministries look to their retreats for a time to get away for spiritual refreshment and to help women grow in relationships with each other. This section will help your team consider the best options for retreats.

DO I NEED A RETREAT SPEAKER?

This is one of the most common questions we receive. Many women's ministries struggle with a budget that limits options. Or you might live in an area not easily accessible without significant travel time and costs. Someone might recommend a speaker, but you personally don't know her and you're anxious about trusting the teaching of your retreat to her. You have limited options, but you have to have a speaker, right?

Not necessarily.

When you plan a women's retreat, of course, you want it to be effective. Effectiveness involves impacting women's lives, and God works in many ways to impact lives. Think outside the box. Here's how.

Let women experience. When people listen to a speaker for extended periods of time, they might be hearing words, but they're not fully experiencing the content of what's being presented. Let them talk to each other, stand up and move around the room, or try an experiment that tests an idea. This means a speaker is replaced by a facilitator, who keeps the energy of the retreat moving.

Give women more. When you're not spending significant money on a speaker, you're able to invest your resources into the women attending your retreat. Pass the savings along to them through reduced costs or scholarships. Invest what you would have spent on a speaker in a service project women work on at the retreat for your community.

Get more women involved. The more others are involved, the more invested they are to invite friends and create an excellent retreat for everyone. Share responsibilities with other women. Women intimidated by speaking to a group will feel more at ease facilitating a retreat session, where the facilitator is minimally involved and women are actively engaged.

Retreats without speakers can significantly impact women's lives. With Group's women's retreat kits, more women get involved in facilitating the retreat, sharing ownership and excitement. Women at the retreat are more involved and engaged. And your retreat becomes a life-changing experience. Check out group.com/womensretreats, and give it a try!

WHAT DO I DO WHEN THE RETREAT IS OVER?

You pour a lot of work into a retreat that lasts only one or two days. Reap the rewards with these simple ideas to follow up with women after your retreat.

Note It! Write a personal note to each woman who attended the retreat. Gather your team together and celebrate the memories as you write notes. Or pre-print basic notes and have everyone on your leadership team sign them assembly- line style.

Share It! Create a brief slideshow of photos to show before or during worship services to celebrate the event. This is a great reminder for women who attended and also piques the interest of those who couldn't make it this year...they won't miss again!

Post It! Put photos from the retreat on your church website or on Facebook. Provide a place on your website or blog where women can share their retreat stories.

Sing It! Coordinate with your Worship Leader to incorporate a couple retreat songs into worship services within 1 to 2 weeks of your retreat to help women remember their experiences.

Talk It! Set up monthly dates/times for women to connect at a local coffee shop to stay in touch. Create a fun bookmark or magnet and insert it into the retreat journal for women to take home as a reminder.

Pray It! Give women the opportunity to stay connected by offering a follow-up Bible study, perfect for continuing relationships and helping women take time for God and each other.

DESIGNED FOR RELATIONSHIPS
With Others

Women's ministry is way more than parties and teas. But upbeat gatherings are great for outreach and for connecting women into deeper relationships. When you reach women with welcoming get-togethers and inspiring small groups, they'll feel comfortable as they connect and begin new friendships. Yes, your goal is to grow women spiritually, so you'll want all women to become involved in studies and service. However, not everyone will begin there, and not everyone will stay there. Connecting with others creates a sense of belonging and trust. Women's events are often the starting point for these.

In this section, we'll explore different kinds of events you and your team can consider. You don't have to offer all of these and certainly not all at once! Discuss your options, your ideas, and your passions. Then choose a place to begin.

IT'S A SNAP!

You'll find super-easy-to-use guides for a wide variety of resources for women's events at group.com/women and at group.com/SNAP.

Girls' Nights Out

Girls' nights out create connections among women. These are what we would consider to be "smaller" events, in that they don't require a lot of decorating, extra planning, or extra work. Think of it as creating a gathering place for women to get together for a night away from home—a little food, a few games, and one or two other simple activities. It's a safe place for women to bring their neighbors, co-workers, family, and friends. It's also an easy way to build community and a sense of belonging in your group.

We like to call these "Girls' Nights Out," but you can call them something else that works for your ministry (and they don't have to be at night!). We've heard of names like Second Saturday (and they meet on the second Saturday of each month), Meet at the Park (and they go to a different community park each month), and so on. It doesn't matter to us what you call these—or if you have any name for them at all! Just be sure you're doing them!

Girls' Nights Out are *not* a place where women sit in chairs and listen to a speaker. Girls' Nights Out let women talk, laugh, and play together as they choose their own experiences. Remember, this is about relationships—not lectures.

Amazingly, when women see they can get together and have fun, they're more likely to make a few new friends, come back, and get involved. These events are great for welcoming women from outside your church and helping them see that following Jesus doesn't mean forgetting how to laugh and love.

HOW OFTEN?

It's up to you and your team! These gatherings usually last about two hours and can be offered on any night of the week. Some women's ministries keep it the same night each time (such as the first Monday of every other month), and some vary it to meet the needs of women's various schedules. Just remember to always promote your Girls' Night Out with enough advance notice that women will be able to make plans to be there.

DECORATIONS

Keep it simple. You do not have to decorate! Keep the focus on creating a welcoming, interactive gathering place. We can easily go overboard on decorations, spending hours planning, shopping, setting up, and breaking down. Encourage your team to enjoy the experience of the Girls' Nights Out as much as the women you're reaching.

FOOD

Again, keep it simple. "Grazing" food such as chips and dip, a veggie tray, a cookie plate from a local bakery, and a couple beverage options is plenty.

THE ACTUAL GATHERING

We encourage you to think outside the box. Try new things. Consider the women you previously haven't been reaching. Allow women to have choices. Here are some things we've found important for Girls' Nights Out gatherings:

- Upbeat music. Choose songs that go along with your theme and have them playing in the background, but not so loudly that conversations are drowned by the music.
- Friendly greeters to help everyone feel welcome and involved.

- Simple activities on tables—such as board games, puzzles, or easy craft projects anyone can do. Give women something easy to join into as they arrive so they're not awkwardly standing around.
- Service project options. If possible, offer a service project that gives women something to do for others.

EASY IDEAS

Talk as a team to come up with fun ideas you haven't tried before. Here are a few we've done that were popular and easy to pull off:

- Board Game Night (or Bunko night)
- Campfire (gather at a location where you can have a bonfire. Hot dogs and s'mores are a must!)
- Birthday Party (celebrate everyone's special day all at once)
- Chick Flicks (popcorn and a movie you've screened ahead of time)
- Show and Tell (let everyone bring something related to a hobby to show others)
- Ice Cream Social (have everyone bring a topping while you provide the ice cream)

Ideas our team has for smaller gatherings that will connect women and help them begin to build friendships:

Over-the-Top Events

Every now and then (no more than twice a year, though!) you might consider offering an "over-the-top" event, reaching into and serving the community by gathering as many women as possible for a time of fun, laughter, and connecting. These are excellent for *outreach* as any woman in your community can come and feel welcomed and at ease right away.

If you decide to try a larger event, you'll need to involve a team of women to plan and pull off these events.

HOW BIG IS BIG?

It's okay to start small and then build. You might start with 15 for your first event, and at your next event have 50. You might start with 4 women and within a year have 12. You might start with 100 and within five years have 700! Pray about what a realistic goal would be for your women's ministry.

Don't get frustrated if women don't start buying tickets until a week or so prior. Advance commitment is an issue for many of us. Sell as many advance tickets as possible, and then allow others to pay at the door. Promote discounted advance-purchase ticket and a higher-price ticket at the door (about $5 more) to encourage early ticket sales.

Pray! Pray! Pray! Remember women's ministry is about creating connections among women so women grow in their relationships with Jesus. If you pour your time and energy into an event and very few women attend but significant connections are made, praise God!

FEE OR FREE?

Realizing that ministries vary in size and personality, we recommend you charge at least $5 but less than $15.

It's hard to find the balance between what attendees perceive as value and the actual value of the event. Where else can they get pampering, food, coffee, and an incredible experience for that price? Going to the movies and just getting popcorn and a soft drink will cost much more than that! Work with your team to determine how much you should budget for each area (food, decorations, publicity, and so on), estimate a cost per woman, and then determine your ticket prices. As your church leadership sees the value of such events, you might be able to build your event budget, so you can keep the costs even lower as you reach women.

WHY CHARGE AT ALL?

"If this is an outreach event, why charge admission?" Great question! Charging admission encourages commitment from those attending, communicates the value of the event, and helps you provide women with an incredible evening. Just because something is outreach doesn't mean it has to be free to everyone who attends.

THE ACTUAL OVER-THE-TOP EVENT

Of course, events are going to look different for different churches and communities, but here's what we've experienced as a few essentials:

- A theme. Be creative!
- Food (not a full meal, just lots of finger foods that relate to the theme if possible).

- Coffee and tea (flavored creamers are a nice touch!).
- Crafts (simple ones that anyone can do and that relate to the theme).
- Games (both "quiet" games such as board and card games and "loud" games such as relays, rowdy contests, line dancing, and so on.)
- Upbeat music.
- Lots of laughter!
- A service project women can join for the evening.
- Friendly greeters to help everyone feel welcome and involved.

Retreats

Yes, we talked about retreats in the section on spiritual growth, but these also have an aspect of connecting women that is so critical, we think it's worth talking about them just a little bit more!

REFRESHING, REVIVING, RESTORING RETREATS

Women in your church and community invest much time and energy into their families, communities, and work. They often sacrifice their own needs for others. While their sacrifices are honorable, they sometimes sacrifice their personal spiritual needs. Women's retreats provide an opportunity for women to be spiritually fed in a setting customized for women's needs. A remarkable retreat includes:

- **Friendships.** When women exchange encouragement, challenges, and stories, they invest in each other. Retreats give women the opportunity to connect and share.

- **Fun.** Women still enjoy giggles…they simply don't take as much time to giggle once they're grown up. Retreats give women the opportunity to relax and enjoy themselves in a casual setting.

- **Faith.** Women are passionate about faith. Retreats give women the opportunity to be challenged to grow and serve according to the desires of God and the needs of the church and community.

  Retreats provide an opportunity for women to spend concentrated time being spiritually fed and encouraged in a casual setting. They're an investment in the lives of women. When you invest in your women, you'll reap benefits of your investment for years to come.

LET US DO THE HEAVY LIFTING

Most women's ministries offer a retreat once a year. Planning retreats can be a lot of work. Group's women's ministry retreat kits (yep—a *kit*!) are made with you in mind. They're designed to help you easily plan a retreat where incredible things will happen. The flexible format allows you to plan a one-day, overnight, or two-day retreat. And because no speaker is required, women are allowed more opportunities for sharing and discovery.

We've made it easy for you so you can offer women of all ages an experience that's relational, personal, and enriching. You'll see friendships formed, and women will go home with life-changing ways to apply the Bible truths they've learned to their own lives.

Plus, we create a new retreat kit every year, so you always have a fresh theme with new content and ideas to attract, involve, and grow your women. Visit group.com/womensretreats for current retreat kit information, including free samples, testimonials, and more.

DESIGNED FOR All Ages

Is your ministry overflowing with women of one age group...but missing women from another? We often make generalizations or form stereotypes about people based on our own experiences. But we also meet people who don't fit into these generalizations or stereotypes. It's important to be aware of our stereotypes, knowing how they limit us, as well as learn how to use some general characteristics of groups of people.

The discussions you and your team have related to different age groups and life stages of women will help you evaluate what you're offering, how you can reach women outside your established group, and be freshly relevant to more women in your church and community.

WHERE ARE THEY?

Ninety-six percent of women's ministry leaders say "reaching younger women" is important to their ministries. The reality is that younger people (men and women) are attending church (and church-related activities) less and less. Want to learn more about reaching them? We recommend the book *Why Nobody Wants to Go to Church Anymore: And How 4 Acts of Love Will Make Your Church Irresistible* by Thom and Joani Schultz.

Let's Talk About Teens

Young women might not overcome negative stereotypes while still in their teen years, but your ministry can plant seeds to help them grow into adulthood with grace and love. Your ministry might not focus on teen girls, but all women's ministries need to understand these young women. Some churches begin inviting high school girls to join in some events and retreats while they're still in these school years to help them transition into adult ministries more easily. Even if you don't include girls at this age, they're only a few years away from joining your ministry. You'll need to be prepared to help them transition and reach them in early adulthood, if not before.

Discuss these questions as a team:

What words would you use to describe teen girls in general?

_____

_____

_____

What do you love about teen girls? What benefits could they bring to our ministry?

_____

_____

_____

How can our ministry help teen girls overcome some of the negative stereotypes often assigned to them?

_____

_____

_____

How can *we* overcome the stereotypes we have of teen girls?

_____

_____

_____

WHY REACH OUT TO TEENAGE WOMEN?

- A huge number of girls drop out of church as they leave youth ministry and move into college and adult ministry. By giving girls a taste of what's coming after high school, they have something to look forward to and are more likely to stay involved in church.

- Relationships are difficult for many teenage girls. There's a lot of gossip, negative pressure, and drama. By creating a place where they can experience healthy relationships, they're more likely to seek and model healthy relationships in their own lives.

- Younger women need guidance to navigate the difficulties of their lives. But they're not likely to reach out to the women who could help them. They need you to reach out to them. You have to make the first step.

HOW CAN OUR MINISTRY REACH TEEN GIRLS?

- Think of reaching out to teen girls as an outreach of your women's ministry. Make basic connections like sending a birthday card to each teen girl.

- Involve teen girls in Girls' Nights Out, retreats, or shared-interest groups. Whether you invite these young women to all of your gatherings, or have specific groups and events set aside for them, you're building relationships and planting seeds for future involvement.

- Multiply your women's ministry by having a connected yet separate teen girls' ministry. Be sure to coordinate all efforts to reach teen girls with your youth ministry.

- Invite one or two younger women to be on your leadership team. Hear from these girls often about what's happening in their lives, what's going on in their schools, and where they need women ahead of them in life to join in.

- Partner with the leadership team from your church's youth ministry. Look for ways to work together in reaching girls.

Let's Talk About Older Women

This is a bit tricky. No one wants to be an "older" woman! Instead of defining this age group, let's assume older women are women who are older than ourselves! Or perhaps as you begin this discussion, your leadership team can create your own definition based on your church demographics.

What words would you use to describe older women in general?

What do you love about the older women in our church? What benefits could they bring to our ministry?

How can our ministry help older women overcome some of the negative stereotypes often assigned to them?

_____

_____

_____

How can we overcome the stereotypes we have of older women?

_____

_____

_____

How can we reach older women through our women's ministry?

_____

_____

_____

WHY REACH OUT TO OLDER WOMEN?

- Older women have a lifetime of experiences to share. Although culture has changed, their relationship experiences and variety of skills can encourage and help women of all life stages.

- Older women need relationships and purpose just as much as every other woman! They need to be befriended and find a place to belong where they can continue to grow in faith.

- Many older women are in a stage of life where they have more time to offer. They are likely to be available for many areas of ministry and can be a great asset to your team.

- These women often have a combination of qualities few others have. In addition to their life experiences, many have long-standing relationships in the church and community. This often allows them to influence key people who can help with reaching the goals of your ministry.

HOW CAN OUR MINISTRY REACH OLDER WOMEN?

- Share you ministry's purpose with older women. Share your passion for reaching women. They likely share the same passion but simply have a different approach!

- Invite older women to become involved in service and ministry. There are so many ways they can be touching the lives of others.

- Minister to older women. Work through your ministry's purpose to discuss how you can meet the needs and involve older women in each of these areas. Invite one or more older women to be on your leadership team so you can hear directly from them about their needs, interests, challenges, and so on. These women might open your eyes to the difficulties of navigating a mountain path at a retreat center, to the challenges they face driving at night or in inclement weather, or to the vast wealth of knowledge they have that they can offer others!

It's Your Turn!

As a leadership team, identify the group or groups of women you think are missing from your ministry or even from your church. Have a brainstorm session together, using the following questions as a guide.

What groups of women do we stereotype, in good and bad ways? (single, moms, divorced, working, and so on.)

_____

_____

_____

How do our own stereotypes affect our ministries?

_____

_____

_____

How can we reach women who are at different life stages?

_____

_____

_____

Why do we want to reach women in these groups?

_____

_____

_____

THE CHILDCARE DILEMMA

If your ministry is attracting women of various life stages, you'll need to address childcare needs at some point. Choose the best options for your ministry and community. Here are several approaches your team can consider.

- Childcare is provided for all women's ministry events and groups. Costs are covered by the church budget, included in event costs, or handled through donations. Childcare providers are moms who take turns, volunteers, professionals from the community, or teens.

- Be sure to protect your church and your children by requiring background checks on all volunteers. Learn more at group.com/shepherdswatch.

- Childcare is provided for specific gatherings. Depending on space and childcare provider availability, childcare might be provided for all events but not Bible study gatherings, or vice versa. Or childcare might be provided only on specific evenings or days.

- Each small group or Bible study group makes its own decision and arrangements concerning childcare instead of relying on the church.

- Women find their own childcare, or a list of possible childcare providers is given to women with a childcare concern.

Including Others

ALL AGES REPRESENTED

One of the best ways to include women of all ages is...to include them! An excellent way to do this is to be sure that each "decade" is represented in your leadership team. This means you should have one woman in her 20s, one in her 30s, one in her 40s, and so on. You might want to begin with a woman in her late teens and invite someone from the oldest group of women in your church too!

When you do this, the women who are on your team will give you ideas and suggestions based on the needs and interests of women their own age, and they'll also invite women near their own age to events, Bible studies, and so on. And when women see that you're hearing from a variety of age groups, they'll know you've been paying attention to them.

ALL AGES SERVING

Another way to get women of all ages involved is to offer opportunities for all ages to serve. For example, could you invite a woman in her early 20s to lead worship at your retreat instead of asking the organist who does it every year? Or pair a woman in her teens and a woman in her 50s to lead a Bible study together. Or have a younger woman create and maintain a website or social networking page for your group. Look for things women of all ages do well, and invite them to serve there.

AGE AND LIFE STAGE

Keep in mind that women who are the same age may not be at the same life stage. For example, some women marry young—others wait. Some have children young. Others wait or never have any children. Some have an empty nest when they're only 40; for others this won't happen until they're in their 60s or even older. This means women are going through different things. Different life stages. If you offer a class for young moms, what will the women who are in that age group who don't have kids do? Will they be left out? Or is there something else you can offer for them?

We're not trying to make life difficult for you—just giving you things to think about. Are you really only reaching out to one group of women with your offerings? Or are you opening your arms to many women? Think about it!

So Many Groups...

We've focused a lot on younger women and older women because that's what women's ministry leaders ask us about the most. How do I reach younger women, and how do I reach older women. Both are important.

But there are many other groups that might be represented in your church. Depending on where you live, what kinds of industry are prominent in your area, the economic structure of your community, and so on, there are many other groups of women you could reach out to intentionally.

For example, if you live in an area with a large college, you might intentionally reach out to college girls. If you're in an area near a military base, you might reach out to women who are serving in the military or wives and mothers of those serving in the military. Consider these groups that might be strong in your area:

- professionals or those in the corporate world
- single moms
- single women without kids
- married without kids
- women in the military
- women with family in the military
- retired women
- grandmothers raising grandchildren
- women recovering from crisis

You can imagine this list could get pretty long! We're not suggesting you have to offer something for every group of women in your church. Just the fact that they're all women may be enough for you and your team! But do be aware of the groups of women represented within the walls of your building and the ones who are represented in your community that might come inside your walls if they were welcomed. Again, something to think about and grapple with as a team!

Lifestyle Mentoring

Many churches tell us they want to start a mentoring program. But there are so many difficulties, such as women who don't like their assigned mentor (or mentee), the fact that many don't think of themselves as mentors, the struggle with finding something that's meaningful for many women to participate in, and so on. This leaves things feeling neither fresh nor vibrant!

That's why we're huge fans of *lifestyle* mentoring instead of a mentoring *program*. What's the difference between mentoring and *lifestyle mentoring*? In *That Makes Two of Us* (Group), authors Connie Witt and Cathi Workman talk about how they share life together. Everyday life, like shopping, cooking, and walking. Mentoring can happen when you simply go out for coffee, catch a movie, drive to the airport together, visit a favorite store, or walk around your neighborhood. Just think of anything two women can do together. Watch for lifestyle connections with other women. It's not time-consuming or expensive. And it's fun!

Recall a woman who impacted your life and helped shape you into the woman you are today.

_____

_____

_____

_____

_____

MYTHS OF MENTORING

We wanted to share with you some highlights from *That Makes Two of Us* to help you start thinking about how lifestyle mentoring might work for women in your church. If this gets your group excited, we recommend you pick up a copy of the book and get started!

MYTH: I MUST BE SMART.

TRUTH: You must be willing to share what you already know. God has taught you tons of stuff along your journey. That's what you must be willing to share with whomever God puts in your path. So what if you don't have an IQ of 180? To be honest, most of the world wouldn't be able to connect with you if you did!

MYTH: IT'S VERY TIME-CONSUMING.

TRUTH: You must be willing to open up your life and allow someone to come along with you. You've got to start seeing your life and your daily schedule as an avenue to build relationships. You don't have to add anything to your schedule. The way to think about mentoring the next generation is to *show* them, not *tell* them. They want to see Jesus in your life. They want to see you walk the walk not just talk the talk. So take them along with you. Take them through life with you.

MYTH: YOUNGER WOMEN DON'T WANT TO HANG OUT WITH ME!

TRUTH: This is totally untrue! Because of the way this generation was raised and the pattern of the previous generation, there is a *longing* to have the influence of older women in their lives. There are so many young women who have little or no relationship with their moms. Or even if they have great relationships with their moms, a lot of the time they aren't living in the same cities or even states where their moms are.

MYTH: I NEED TO KNOW THE BIBLE BETTER.

TRUTH: You need to be willing and ready to share what you've already learned. Yes, we all need to continue growing and learning, but to decide not to invest in the next generation because we aren't Billy Graham isn't really acceptable. Think about it: Do you know the Bible better now than you did last year? What about now compared to two years ago? Or five years ago? If you've attended one or two church services, the answer should be yes! So share what you know. God has taught you more than you think. We tend to focus on what we don't know more than what we do know.

MYTH: I DON'T HAVE ANY CURRICULUM.

TRUTH: Your life is your curriculum. God wants to use your experiences…your successes…your failures…your hurts…your life. You have plenty of material to use to impact the life of someone else.

MYTH: I DON'T HAVE ANYTHING TO OFFER.

TRUTH: You have everything to offer. You have your time, your love, your laughter, your skills, your experience, your knowledge, your hugs, your tears…*you!*

Adapted from *That Makes Two of Us* (Group Publishing).

There was a lot to digest in this section! What are our team thoughts on how to move ahead with this info in mind?

_____

_____

_____

_____

CELEBRATING Success!

You can see that this process is not a DIY (do it yourself) improvement but both a DIWG and DIWT (do it with God and do it with team) process!

A final thought before we wrap up this book: Be sure to take time to celebrate success. When a woman makes a decision to follow Jesus—celebrate! When a new person comes to your church and finds community—celebrate! When more women come to an event than you ever imagined—celebrate! Gather the stories of what's happening and how God is working through your ministry and share them! Celebrate all that God is doing!

Thanks for taking the time to work through this process with your team. Because of your care and work, this ministry is stronger and more effective. Thanks for caring about the personal and spiritual growth of women in your church and community. Thanks for making a difference!